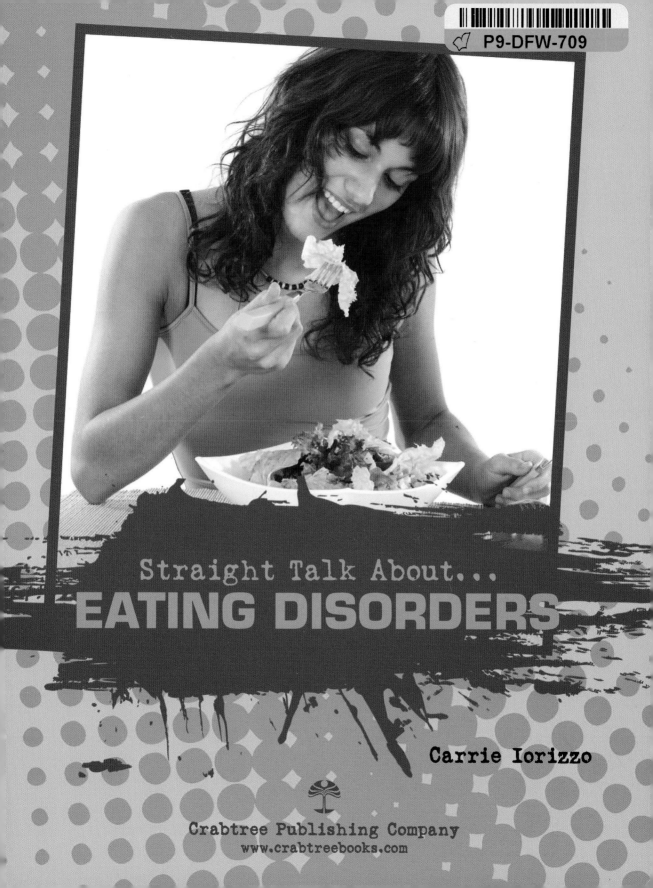

Straight Talk About...
EATING DISORDERS

Carrie Iorizzo

Crabtree Publishing Company
www.crabtreebooks.com

Straight Talk About...

Developed and produced by: Netscribes Inc.

Author: Carrie Iorizzo

Publishing plan research and development:
Sean Charlebois, Reagan Miller
Crabtree Publishing Company

Project Controller: Sandeep Kumar G

Editorial director: Kathy Middleton

Editors: John Perritano, Molly Aloian

Proofreader: Kathy Middleton

Art director: Dibakar Acharjee

Designer: Shruti Aggarwal

Cover design: Margaret Amy Salter

Production coordinator and
prepress technician: Margaret Amy Salter

Print coordinators: Katherine Berti,
Margaret Amy Salter

Consultant: Carla Lundblade, M.S., L.P.C., N.C.C.

Photographs:
Cover: Jaimie Duplass/Shutterstock; Title Page: Gelpi JM/Shutterstock Inc.; p.4: Piotr Marcinski/Shutterstock Inc.; p.6: Kekyalyaynen/Shutterstock Inc.; p.8: Monkey Business Images/Shutterstock Inc.; p.9: Mark Herreid / Shutterstock Inc.; p.10: Catalin Petolea/ Shutterstock Inc.; p.13: Yuri Arcurs/Shutterstock Inc.; p.14: Monkey Business Images/Shutterstock Inc.; p.15: NotarYES/ Shutterstock Inc.; p.16: Elena Elisseeva/Shutterstock Inc.; p.19: Shutterstock Inc.; p.20: Stuart Monk/ Shutterstock Inc.; p.22: Orhan Cam/Shutterstock Inc.; p.24: Piotr Marcinski/Shutterstock Inc.; p.25: PHOTO FUN/Shutterstock Inc.; p.26: Sergey Peterman/ Shutterstock Inc.; p.28: Daniel_Dash/Shutterstock Inc.; p.31: Ariwasabi/Shutterstock Inc.; p.32: Martin Allinger/Shutterstock Inc.; p.34: OLJ Studio/ Shutterstock Inc.; p.35: Kolobrod/Shutterstock Inc.; p.36: REATISTA/Shutterstock Inc.; p.38.1: Sweet November studio/Shutterstock Inc.; p.38.2: TrotzOlga/ Shutterstock Inc.; p.40: pedalist/Shutterstock Inc.; p.42:wrangler/Shutterstock Inc.

Library and Archives Canada Cataloguing in Publication

Iorizzo, Carrie
    Eating disorders / Carrie Iorizzo.

(Straight talk about--)
Includes index.
Issued also in electronic format.
ISBN 978-0-7787-2183-3 (bound).--ISBN 978-0-7787-2190-1 (pbk.)

    1. Eating disorders--Juvenile literature. I. Title. II. Series: Straight talk about-- (St. Catharines, Ont.)

RC552.E18I67 2013   j616.85'26   C2013-900981-7

Library of Congress Cataloging-in-Publication Data

Iorizzo, Carrie.
  Eating disorders / Carrie Iorizzo.
      pages cm -- (Straight talk about)
  Includes index.
   ISBN 978-0-7787-2183-3 (reinforced library binding) --
  ISBN 978-0-7787-2190-1 (pbk.) -- ISBN 978-1-4271-9066-6
  (electronic pdf) -- ISBN 978-1-4271-9120-5 (electronic html)
  1. Eating disorders--Juvenile literature. 2. Eating disorders in
  adolescence--Juvenile literature. 3. Self-perception--Juvenile
  literature. I. Title.

  RC552.E18I587 2013
  616.85'26--dc23
                                    2013004642

Crabtree Publishing Company

www.crabtreebooks.com   1-800-387-7650

Printed in the USA/052013/JA20130412

Published in Canada
Crabtree Publishing
616 Welland Ave.
St. Catharines, ON
L2M 5V6

Published in the United States
Crabtree Publishing
PMB 59051
350 Fifth Avenue, 59th Floor
New York, New York 10118

Published in the United Kingdom
Crabtree Publishing
Maritime House
Basin Road North, Hove
BN41 1WR

Published in Australia
Crabtree Publishing
3 Charles Street
Coburg North
VIC, 3058

CONTENTS

Nicki stood naked in front of the full-length mirror in the bathroom. No matter how many times she threw up, she just couldn't get rid of that fat blob on her hips.

Nicki stepped on the scale and watched the red needle hover over the 95-pound mark. *Ninety-five pounds—I'm such a fat slob! I'm pathetic. I ate three pieces of chocolate cake, a bag of barbecue chips, and all the leftover potato salad.*

Nicki rifled through a drawer until she found the *Ipecac*. Without measuring, she tipped her head back and drained the dark liquid from the bottle.

She sat on the toilet seat and waited. Soon, the Ipecac would start to work, and all that food would be down the toilet. *Never again*, she promised. *I'll never eat again. But mom was right. I'm a pig when it comes to food.* Nicki braced herself as her stomach began to churn. She began to vomit. Her throat was always sore from puking, almost as sore as her stomach. *This time would be different*, she promised. *No more food.*

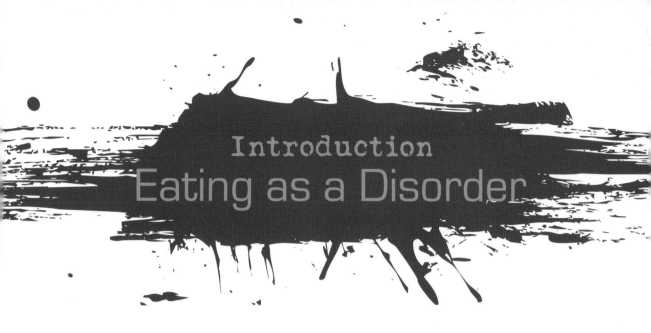

Introduction
Eating as a Disorder

Nicki, like millions of others, has an eating disorder. An eating disorder is a type of mental illness. Eating disorders are complicated. Scientists and researchers have identified some of the factors that play a role in eating disorders, also known as ED. Some of those factors include: family environment, cultural background, *genes*, peer pressure, and stress.

There are three main types of eating disorders: anorexia nervosa, bulimia nervosa, and compulsive-eating disorder. Other eating disorders that are not as well known include purging disorder, night-eating syndrome, and orthorexia, in which a person obsesses about eating healthy foods.

When most people think about eating disorders they think of girls like Nicki. But eating disorders affect both girls and boys. Some studies say boys are good at hiding an eating disorder. It's estimated that there are more than a million adolescent boys in the United States who suffer from eating disorders.

"It started out in my sophomore year at high school. I just wanted to get healthy and lose five pounds. It wasn't long before it became an obsession. I got to such a low weight my hair was falling out in clumps." Tammy, aged 17.

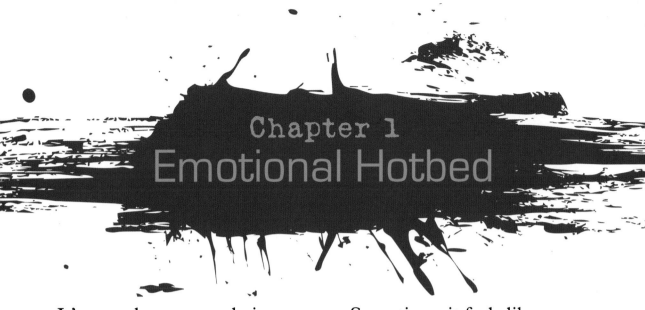

Chapter 1
Emotional Hotbed

It's not always easy being young. Sometimes it feels like no one is listening. Nothing you wear looks good. Your biceps just won't pop. No one understands.

Such feelings are normal. If these feelings become extreme, they might affect your daily routine and cause stress and poor health. Self-critical thoughts, negative feelings about body image, food, and weight gain, might be the beginnings of an eating disorder.

ED can start out innocently. You might want to drop five pounds to fit into a new bathing suit or just want to eat healthier and work on those abdominal muscles. These are all great ideas, but when mixed with a fatal dash of poor self-esteem, identity issues, and problems at home or school, you may find yourself developing a serious health issue.

Food becomes a crutch that helps you deal with larger issues that are often too hard to face, too painful to deal with, or just too embarrassing.

Big Problem

Eating disorders in the United States affect two kids out of every 100, including boys. In Canada, 37 percent of Grade 9 girls and 40 percent of Grade 10 girls think they're too fat. Twenty-five percent of adolescent boys get teased about their weight at school and at home. In 2002, 1.5 percent of all Canadian women between the ages of 15 and 24 had an eating disorder.

Eating can be fun, but eating disorders are a problem both males and females face each day.

By the Numbers

- In the United States, almost 24 million people have an eating disorder.
- One study estimates that 0.9 percent of females and 0.3 percent of all males that have anorexia nervosa will have it their entire lives. Of those who suffer from bulimia nervosa, 1.5 percent of females and 0.5 percent of males will deal with it their entire lives.
- In Canada, about 10 to 20 percent of people with eating disorders die from medical problems.

What's Healthy?

What does it mean to be healthy? First, being healthy means eating when you're hungry and making smart food choices every day.

Being healthy also means exercising for one hour a day, but not overdoing it. It means eating five servings—about 2.5 cups (600 mL)—of fruits and vegetables each day. It means choosing whole grains and lean proteins. It involves avoiding fast foods, fatty foods, and sugary foods and drinks.

Maintaining a nutritious diet coupled with moderate exercise contributes to healthy weight management.

It also means treating yourself on occasion. Eating a piece of chocolate cake now and then can make just about any day perfect.

The American Heart Association recommends that girls between the ages of 9 and 13 consume 1,600 **calories** a day. Girls between the ages of 14 to 18 should eat 1,800 calories a day. For boys between 9 and 13, the suggested calorie amount is 1,800. For those between the ages of 14 to 18, it's 2,200 calories per day.

If you're on a sports team or on the go all the time, you should eat a little more.

"It all began in the 7th grade. My face turned into a pizza, and I began to gain weight. I didn't like myself, or anyone else, for that matter. I became depressed and suicidal. I was just the "fat girl."
Jami, aged 15.

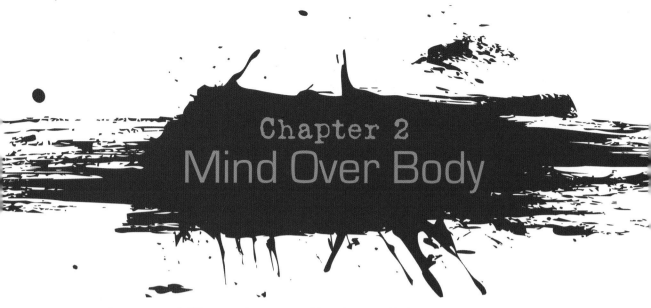

Chapter 2
Mind Over Body

A mental illness is a medical condition involving the mind. Decades ago, people with mental illnesses were shunned by society. They were often locked away in special institutions where they received little treatment. Today, we understand that good mental health is just as important as being in good physical health. Having a mental illness means you have a treatable condition.

ED, like any other mental illness, can change the way you think, how you act, and how you behave. Having an eating disorder can sometimes make it difficult to cope with simple things, such as getting up in the morning, going to school, hanging with your friends, or helping around the house. It can also affect your mood and how you feel about yourself. Having ED is nothing to be ashamed of, though. With help, it can be treated.

Danger Zone

Age and gender are two of the main risk factors when it comes to developing ED. Preteens, teens, and young adults are more at risk of developing eating disorders than older people. However, eating disorders are becoming common in younger children and older adults. Moreover, females are more at risk than males. The University of Maryland Medical Center estimates that 7 million females and 1 million males in the United States have an eating disorders.

Another risk factor is **ethnicity**. Although eating disorders occur in every race and culture, Caucasian, or white, females tend to have the highest risk.

Why is that? Television, movies, magazines, the Internet, advertising, and peer pressure all combine to make young people sensitive about their body images. The constant images of attractive models and thin movie stars can make most of us feel self-conscious about the shape of our bodies.

By the Numbers

- Almost 50 percent of people with eating disorders suffer from depression.
- Only 1 out of 10 people with an eating disorder seeks therapy.
- In the United States, almost 24 million people have some form of eating disorder.
- Eating disorders are the cause of more deaths than any other mental illness.

Source: National Association of Anorexia Nervosa and Associated Disorders

12

More Factors

Certain personality traits, including low self-esteem, the fear of losing control, inappropriate self-discipline, dependency, and the inability to interact with others, can be contributing factors to ED. Some mental illnesses, such as anxiety disorders, depression, and **oppositional defiant disorder**, a condition in which a person is aggressive to anyone in authority, are also associated with eating disorders.

A person might also be **genetically predisposed** to an eating disorder. Researchers have found that if one identical twin has an eating disorder, the other twin will likely suffer from it, too. They also found that people with relatives who have anorexia are eight times more likely to develop the condition than a person who does not have a relative with ED. Scientists have also linked a specific **chromosome**, called chromosome 10, to bulimia and **obesity**. A certain protein in the brain may also put some people at risk.

Although there is no one cause for ED, a preoccupation with your body and weight is high on the list. Many other causes are related to family influences.

Obsession with body shape is common in most eating disorders, as is intense fear of gaining weight and preoccupation with food.

13

All in the Family

Studies have found that girls between the ages of 9 and 10 usually go on diets at the insistence of their mothers. If mom had, or has, an eating disorder, her daughter or daughters will probably have an eating disorder, too. Sexual abuse by family members can also trigger eating disorders in females. Researchers have also found that young boys are heavily influenced by their fathers' disapproval of their weight.

Children whose parents abuse drugs and alcohol often use food as a way to feel in control of their lives. Some teens might suffer from eating disorders if obesity runs in the family.

While the environment in which a person lives plays a role in developing an eating disorder, medical problems are also to blame. Abnormalities in the brain's hypothalamus, which controls behavior, or the amygdala, which plays a role in depression and anxiety, often contribute to the onset of eating disorders. Moreover, hormones that affect stress, appetite, hunger, and metabolism, have an effect.

Family environment is often a good indication of whether you will be stricken with an eating disorder.

Warning Signs

Sometimes it's hard to know if a person has an eating disorder. Each has specific symptoms, but here are some general signs to look for:

Getting help is important for anyone suffering from an eating disorder.

- looking too thin
- tired all the time
- wearing baggy clothes that do not fit properly
- always making excuses to avoid meals and eating
- constant preoccupation with food
- extremely afraid of gaining weight
- concerned about body shape
- avoiding friends and fun activities
- obsessed with exercising
- hiding food
- throwing away uneaten meals
- tiredness, dizziness, and fainting
- vomiting after eating
- swollen jawline, bloodshot eyes, calluses on the knuckles—all indications of vomiting
- always cold, even when it's warm
- irregular, or absent, monthly **menstrual** periods
- moody, withdrawn, secretive, irritable, or depressed

"I remember looking at the scale--115 pounds, and I wanted to be 100 pounds. I ate nothing and started drinking water and exercising too much. One day, when I was running cross country, I passed out. An ambulance took me to the hospital. Doctors said I had anorexia." Anonymous, aged 16.

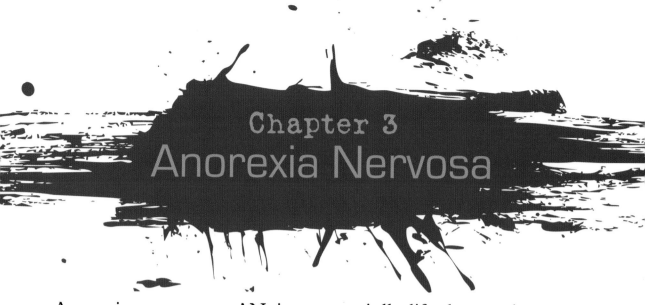

Chapter 3
Anorexia Nervosa

Anorexia nervosa, or AN, is a potentially life-threatening mental illness. It is categorized by severe weight loss caused by self-starvation. People with AN are frightened about gaining weight. They will go to great lengths to maintain a body weight much lower than what is healthy for their age and height.

People suffering from AN not only have the intense fear of gaining weight, but they have distorted perceptions of their bodies. They often deny that they are hungry. Still, anorexic people remain preoccupied with food and often cook for themselves and others.

AN affects both males and females, although more girls than boys suffer from the disorder.

The Perfect Body?

Although anorexia centers on food, its roots go much deeper as a person tries to gain control and to achieve the so-called "perfect body." They regulate their food intake by using **laxatives**, and **diuretics**, or by exercising excessively.

There are two subtypes of anorexia. Restricting anorexia is the classic form of the condition, in which people maintain a low body weight by carefully regulating the foods they eat. They might constantly exercise or starve themselves to bring their weight down.

Binging (and **purging**) is another type of anorexia. A binger will eat large quantities of food and then purge, or force themselves, to vomit.

White females are more likely to suffer from anorexia than any other group. About 10 percent of young males will also develop anorexia.

Eating disorders, such as anorexia, tend to run in families, especially those that are goal-oriented. How do you know if you or someone you love has anorexia? Some of the risk factors include:

- being worried about your weight and body shape
- having anxiety as a child
- having eating problems as a very young child

Researchers also believe that a person's genetic make-up might play a role in developing anorexia.

Tell-Tale Signs

The most recognizable symptom of anorexia is severe weight loss. However, excessively thin arms and legs with little muscle tone or body fat, prominent cheek and **clavicle** bones, sunken eyes that have dark circles, brittle nails, and baggy clothes, are also indications that a person is suffering from anorexia. Some other tell-tale signs might be:

- not eating around other people
- obsessed with exercising, even if you're sick or hurt
- being petrified of gaining weight
- not menstruating for three months
- eating only very small amounts of food
- playing with food on the plate
- use of laxatives, diet pills, and diuretics
- depression, low self-esteem and self-worth
- feeling of having no control over your life
- tired all the time
- forgetful
- confused
- dry, blotchy, or yellow skin covered by soft hair
- always cold, even in warm weather
- weak with little body strength
- dry mouth

Among adolescent females, anorexia is the third most common **chronic** ailment. If not treated early, anorexia can have fatal consequences.

Body Breakdown

Anorexia, like other eating disorders, is usually triggered by a traumatic event such as divorce, death, or some form of physical or sexual abuse. The event leaves people feeling out of control. As a result, they use their bodies to gain back the control they believe they have lost.

People with AN are often depressed and feel little self-worth. They don't like their bodies. They don't like themselves.

Even though people with anorexia are extremely **undernourished**, they still think they are fat and will try to lose more weight to achieve what they believe is the perfect body weight.

The weight loss can become so severe that they have little or no fat left on their bodies. Yet, anorexia sufferers will still feel they need to lose more. Fat is essential for the body to function properly. Without fat, which is stored in cells, some vitamins can't be absorbed, and vital organs aren't protected from injury. Consequently, the various systems in the body begin to fail, including the **circulatory system**.

Although too much body fat can be unhealthy, your body still needs the fat stored in cells to function.

How Low Can You Go?

Anorexia can stop girls from menstruating. It can cause bones to become brittle and break easily. Kidneys can fail and the heart might beat abnormally.

Anorexia can also impact the circulatory system. People with anorexia can become anemic. This means that the blood is unable to carry enough oxygen to the organs, cells, and brain. As a result, they feel very tired. They cannot think clearly. Their emotional problems seem to get worse.

The more weight a person loses, the more serious the problem. While the solution might sound easy—just eat, right?—it is extremely complicated.

Anorexia nervosa is dangerous and can lead to death. The body can literally shut itself down.

Doctors consider anorexia nervosa the most dangerous of all eating disorders. Up to 10 percent of anorexic people die from medical complications. A person who undergoes successful treatment, however, still runs the risk of getting the condition later in life. That's why life-long treatment might be necessary to keep the illness in check.

By the Numbers

- One of the reasons boys are unlikely to seek help for an eating disorder is because boys believe only girls can suffer from the condition.
- Almost 14 percent of gay men suffer from bulimia and 20 percent from anorexia.

Source: National Association of Anorexia Nervosa and Associated Disorders

"First, I tried the usual dieting. I ate a lot of canned soup. Nothing worked. I needed to do something else. I wanted to become skinny and sexy, just like the models in the magazines. I forced myself to vomit." Tianna, aged 14.

Chapter 4
Bulimia Nervosa

Bulimia nervosa, or BN, is an eating disorder in which a person consumes large amounts of food and then purges to avoid gaining weight. Like anorexia nervosa, bulimia is a mental disorder. The American Psychiatric Association classifies bulimics as those who binge, or engage in uncontrolled eating, and purging at least twice a week for three months.

Bulimics purge in a variety of ways. They use diuretics, laxatives, fasting, over-exercising, and self-induced vomiting. Bulimia can be triggered by any number of emotional or physical traumas including depression, a death in the family, a divorce or separation, or a physical assault.

Bulimics cannot stop themselves from eating. Yet, when they do eat, they'll binge on foods that are low in nutrition and high in calories. After binging, bulimics feel guilty for eating too much. They purge the food that they have ingested.

The Need to Purge

Bulimics often use laxatives or give themselves **enemas**. Fasting, or not eating, is another way they control weight. However, fasting can also lead to a number of health problems, including malnutrition and **dehydration**.

After they purge, bulimics become so hungry that they binge again, repeating a vicious cycle. Boys suffering from bulimia will exercise excessively, even more than girls. Yet, the most common way to purge is by self-induced vomiting. Excessive vomiting can leave the body depleted of vital nutrients. It can leave you dehydrated. It can also give you a sore throat as the acidic juices of the stomach irritate the **esophagus**.

Most bulimics self-induce vomiting by sticking their fingers down their throat, or drinking Ipecac syrup. However it's done, constant vomiting can lead to broken blood vessels

on your face and in the whites of your eyes. It can also cause problems with your teeth, throat, and heart, and leave your body chemically imbalanced. Moreover, purging leaves a person feeling more depressed than they did in the first place.

Induced vomiting, also known as purging, is a sign of an eating disorder.

What's the Difference?

Although BN and AN are similar, there are some significant differences. Those with anorexia focus on losing weight. Those with bulimia can be of normal body weight, or even higher than normal body weight.

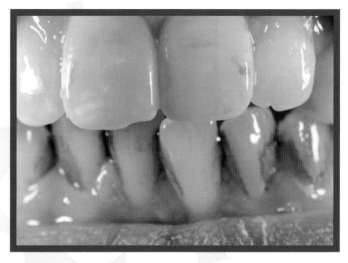

This picture shows the damage that excessive vomiting can do to the teeth.

Bulimic people may fast for a day or so, whereas anorexic people may fast for long periods.

In addition, bulimics tend to be more outgoing than those with AN. Bulimics are very secretive about their purging and eating habits. People with bulimia may be depressed, moody, and impulsive. Anorexia is usually associated with **obsessive-compulsive** behavior, a mental illness characterized by thoughts that produce uneasiness, fear, or worry. People with anorexia do not want to lose control.

There are some medical differences between the two disorders, as well. Anorexic girls tend to stop getting their periods, while bulimic girls tend to have irregular periods. Those suffering from bulimia tend to have more dental issues. The stomach's **hydrochloric acid** can break down the enamel on the teeth during excessive vomiting.

I've Got a Secret

Secrecy is the cornerstone of bulimia. Bulimic people go to great lengths to keep their binging and purging private. Some may hide food in their bedrooms and then eat at night, or when no one is home. Others might eat at fast food restaurants or in their cars.

Purging is also kept secret. People with bulimia will often excuse themselves from class and go to the bathroom to vomit. They will also hide their use of laxatives or enemas.

The causes of BN are not clear. Researchers believe bulimia is associated with a variety of factors, including a family's cultural beliefs about how a boy or girl should look; the media's perception of a beautiful body; how a person feels about his or her body; family problems; and mental health issues. BN is seen a lot in young males and females who are in entertainment and modeling.

Bulimia sufferers are prone to secrecy, especially about how much food they eat.

Signs and Symptoms

There are numerous signs and symptoms of bulimia. If you think you or a friend might have bulimia, these are the signs to look for:

- overwhelming fear of gaining weight
- constant dieting with little success
- constant unhappiness with body size and shape
- frequent episodes of eating large amounts of food, usually low in nutrition and high in **carbohydrates**
- forced vomiting
- excessive exercising
- bad breath, sore mouth and throat, teeth that are losing their enamel, excessive tooth decay
- excessive burping, **flatulence**, nausea, stomach pain
- compulsive weighing, pinching of body fat, constant body measuring

Not everyone suffering from bulimia will have all the medical and physical complications, but they are likely to have a number of them.

By the Numbers

Studies show that bulimic people usually have at least one obese parent. They also have a 35 percent likelihood of having been sexually abused.

Source: National Criminal Justice Reference Service

"The numbers of males with eating disorders have shown a drastic increase since the 1980s. How men look is becoming as important in the media as how young women look." Carla, clinical therapist.

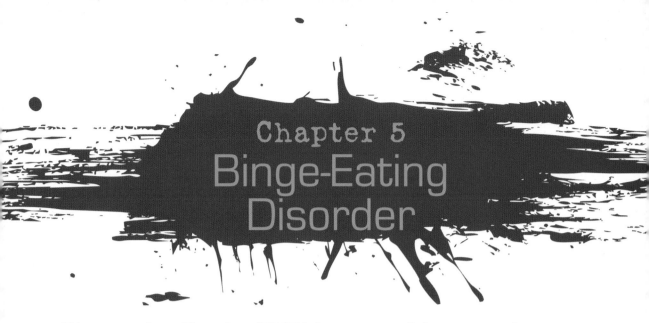

Chapter 5
Binge-Eating Disorder

Binge-eating disorder (BED) is a compulsive overeating disorder. Although BED is a lot like bulimia nervosa, there is no purging or excessive exercising involved. The affliction affects girls and boys, but is more often seen in females.

People who suffer from BED consume upwards of 15,000 calories during a binging session. Consider that an average, healthy adult male in his 30s needs between 2,500 and 3,000 calories per day.

Here are some characteristics of a binge eater:

• eating large amounts of food and promising never to do it again
• eating fast as they binge
• eating even after having a full meal
• expert at hoarding food, eating alone, and in secret

Researchers say your chances of having a binge-eating disorder are higher if there is someone in your family who had, or has one, too.

Mental Health Issues

Males and females who have BED tend to have impulsive personalities. In other words, they tend to act before thinking. There is also an association between BED and depression, low self-esteem, and low self-worth.

Often, those afflicted with BED have a history of substance abuse. In addition, many BED sufferers have high levels of stress. They find it hard to cope with negative emotions such as shame, self-loathing, boredom, worry, and anger. Such feelings can sometimes lead to suicidal thoughts.

Medical Problems

Physical complications associated with binge-eating disorder can be life-threatening. There is a high risk for teenagers to develop type 2 diabetes, high blood pressure, high cholesterol, heart disease, gallbladder disease, and other issues. BED is also linked to some types of cancer. Those with BED are also likely to suffer from joint and muscle pain, insomnia, menstruation problems, and headaches. If not treated, BED can be a lifelong problem.

Up and Down

So-called yo-yo dieting, or cyclical dieting, is one of the characteristics in the BED cycle. Yo-yo dieting is characterized by dieting or fasting, and then regaining the lost weight, if not more.

A University of California study of overweight women found that while yo-yo dieting quickly produces fast weight loss, subsequent dieting did not have the same results. In fact, the more a person dieted, the less weight they lost each time, and the harder it was to keep the pounds off.

Moreover, dieters put the weight on faster. The study recommended that no matter what a person weighs, it is important to strive for a healthy lifestyle. The key is to eat healthy foods in moderate amounts and exercise regularly.

Those suffering from eating disorders often crave foods that are not healthy, such as hamburgers, hot dogs, pizza, and potato chips.

"I realized exercising was taking up too much of my life and making me too stressed out. That's when I started to think that there was something more wrong than just depression." Billy, aged 15.

Chapter 6
Other Eating Disorders

Many people have heard of bulimia or anorexia. But, there are other, lesser-known eating disorders. Medical professionals often lump these conditions into a category called Eating Disorder Not Otherwise Named, or EDNON for short.

But there are other, lesser-known eating disorders. Eating disorders are complex. Many are a mix of anorexia, bulimia, and BED. Others, however, are completely unique.

Purging disorder (PD) is a common ED. It has attributes of bulimia nervosa. Those suffering from PD use diuretics, laxatives, enemas, and diet pills. Like bulimia, PD involves vomiting. The causes of the two are similar. According to some researchers, PD might actually be more common than both anorexia and bulimia.

Medical problems arising from PD depend on the method of purging. People who vomit often can damage their digestive tracts. If they use laxatives or enemas, they could suffer from severe diarrhea or **constipation**.

Night-Eating Syndrome (NES)

Night-eating syndrome is much more serious than just raiding the fridge at night. It affects people who suffer from anxiety and depression. People with NES will wake up in the morning not feeling hungry. They eat very little during the day. Once they go to bed, however, things change. They constantly wake up to eat.

Orthorexia Nervosa (ON)

Orthorexia nervosa is an obsession with eating foods of only the healthiest quality. The name comes from the Greek words "ortho," which means straight, and "orexia," which means appetite. While it is good to eat nutritious foods, people with orthorexia go overboard. If they eat anything else, they feel guilty and ashamed.

People with orthorexia are so obsessed with eating healthy that they limit their food intake to the point where they begin to starve themselves. Their bodies will eventually shut down. The kidneys will stop working, and the heart might begin to beat irregularly. Orthorexia can be fatal.

Eating nutritious meals is essential for good health, but when it becomes an obsession, it can be deadly.

Adonis Rising

The media often uses the term "manorexia" to describe male eating disorders. Although researchers believe 1 million males in the United States suffer from anorexia, most experts say this estimate is too low. In fact, the number might be as high as 1 in 4.

Some males with eating disorders will exercise excessively to achieve the "perfect body."

Athletic males have a higher risk of developing ED than non-athletic males. Guys who participate in gymnastics, running, figure skating, crew, and wrestling, have an even higher risk than other athletes. That's because these sports require leaner bodies. To develop muscles, males might resort to:

- eating only high-protein foods or supplements
- taking **ephedrine**
- using illegal **steroids**
- using food supplements to decrease appetite

A male preoccupied with not feeling muscular suffers from **muscle dysmorphia**, also known as the Adonis Complex.

I knew, with Billy, something was not right...
He was cutting himself off from his friends, he
was fussy about his food, and he was losing weight
very quickly." Billy's mom.

Chapter 7
Love Your Body

There's an old song your parents or grandparents might know. Its lyrics say "love the one you're with." Yet, you're the person you are with most of the time. Loving yourself is often difficult. At the end of the day, however, loving yourself is the only path to a healthy lifestyle.

Good self-esteem and a good body image can go a long way in how you feel about yourself. Self-esteem is how you think about yourself, and how you respect and value who you are. Body image plays an important role in self-esteem.

People suffering from eating disorders find it very difficult to love their bodies. They feel they are too fat, too big, not muscular enough, not strong enough. They believe their bodies lack the features of what desirable bodies are supposed to look like. Their self-worth is attached to this negative picture, which adds to their feelings of poor self-esteem.

Media Influences

Researchers believe that there are a number of factors that can cause people to have low self-esteem and negative self-images. The media, including TV, magazines, and the Internet, is often the biggest problem. The portrayal of Photoshopped, super-thin models, actresses, and muscle-bound jocks, makes many adolescents believe that this is what a normal body should look like.

The media's portrayal of the perfect body is so influential it can cause some people to develop eating disorders.

An interesting study of teenage girls on the South Pacific island of Fiji showed that the introduction of television in 1995 resulted in 15 percent of the girls inducing vomiting to lose weight. In addition, 29 percent were at risk of developing an eating disorder. Another 69 percent began dieting.

This may not seem unusual except that, in the Fijian culture, fat is considered beautiful. That all changed when television came to the island. The girls that were in the study said they wanted to be just like the thin actresses on their favorite shows.

By 2007, 45 percent of the girls said they used laxatives and had purged by vomiting. Also, 25 percent had considered suicide.

Bad Influences

Many people in the entertainment industry believe that having buff, thin bodies will help make them successful. Dance coaches often scold their students about their weight, forcing them to become thinner and more flexible.

In sports, coaches sometimes pressure athletes to become stronger and more muscular. Competition can often trigger an eating disorder.

Peer pressure can also cause an eating disorder. Smoking to keep from eating, fad diets, stimulants, diet pills, and exercising past exertion, all lead to unhealthy eating habits. A joke by a friend about looking fat, or a sibling's nasty comment can be enough to push someone with low self-esteem over the edge and into the pit of an ED.

What is a Healthy Body?

Maintaining a healthy body weight for your height by eating balanced and nutritious meals, along with moderate exercise and good mental health, goes a long way to boosting your self-esteem.

Keeping fit mentally is as important as good physical health. If you're feeling down, discouraged, or bad about yourself, don't wait for those feelings to get out of hand. Talk to a health professional, a school counselor, or trusted adult.

"When I was on the wrestling team, I wouldn't eat more than a couple of pieces of bread a day. I'd carry around a water bottle, even to class, just to spit in to lose water weight. I'd lose a couple [of] pounds a day that way so I could make my weight class." James, aged 21.

Chapter 8
Seeking Help

Doing something about an eating disorder can be difficult. First, you may not believe you are sick. Second, who can you trust? Third, what will happen to you if you tell someone?

Information is power. Before unhealthy eating habits, poor nutrition, and low-self esteem become too hard for you to handle, get help. If someone you know has an eating disorder, offer to help before the problem gets out of hand.

Educate yourself on eating disorders. Read everything you can on the subject. Find out where to get help. Talk to someone you trust. If you wish, look for organizations and agencies that will keep your information anonymous. It's important to get help as soon as possible. Reach out to a friend, the school nurse, or the principal. Help start a program that provides information about eating disorders in your school or community. Encourage a friend to talk and to get help before an eating disorder develops.

Reaching Out

The first and hardest step is to admit you have a problem. The second step is to realize that trying to overcome the problem on your own is very complicated. You need to ask for help.

Find someone who will be understanding and supportive of your situation—a person who will not judge or criticize you. Look for someone you feel comfortable talking to and that you know will give you sound advice.

Help a Friend

You may have a friend or a sibling who is keeping an eating disorder secret, but keeping this secret will not help. Try to approach the situation in an understanding way. Finding the right words to start the conversation can be hard. Try some of these opening lines:

- "I really care about you. Was that you vomiting after supper? Are you all right?"
- "It frightens me when I hear you talk about using laxatives (diuretics, diet pills, enemas)."
- "I know it's hard to talk to mom and dad, but you can talk to me."

You're not helping your friend by not saying something. ED is a serious condition that can kill.

Recovery

Once you have seen a doctor and been diagnosed with an eating disorder, you will experience many different emotions. You might respond with anger, frustration, or fear. You may feel relieved, anxious, or hopeful.

You might also find that you have another mental health issue. You might be suffering from depression, obsessive-compulsive disorder, or **avoidant personality disorder**. Don't fret. There is good news. These illnesses are treatable, as is ED. During treatment you will learn the triggers of your eating disorder. You'll learn about yourself and the challenges you face.

You might participate in a support group where you can share your feelings with others. The goal is to develop a healthy body image and boost your feelings of self-esteem and self-worth.

A Lifelong Commitment

The time it takes for a person to recover is different for each individual. The sooner you start, the shorter the recovery time.

Relapses are a normal part of recovery. That's why it's important for you to remain focused and know that you will get past the setback. A lifelong commitment to eating nutritious food, moderate exercise, and healthy eating habits will play an important role in your recovery. Developing coping strategies will help you get through stressful times.

Hot Topics
Q&A

I don't want to eat all the time. Is that an eating disorder?

A: If your eating patterns are causing you to feel bad about yourself, you may want to talk to someone about it. Unusual eating patterns are not uncommon. They are called disordered eating. Seeking counseling can help you better understand the relationship you have with eating and answer your concerns.

Do eating disorders affect minorities?

A: Yes. Because only white females were studied by researchers for many years, it was thought that eating disorders were a predominantly middle-class, female, Caucasian condition. However, more recent studies using a broader base of people, including males, African Americans, Latinos, Asian Americans, and Native Americans, have given researchers a broader picture of how ED affects other groups.

My brother has ED. He's getting help, but it's so hard to watch him like this. Are there any programs for me and my family to help us get through this with him?

A: Talk to the healthcare professional that is helping your brother. Ask him or her to refer you and your family to a counselor, or to suggest a support group.

My friend is getting so skinny. But I'm not sure she has an eating disorder. She has lunch with me every day and eats as much as I do.

A: Even if your friend is eating, she is still becoming dangerously undernourished. Does your friend excuse herself to go to the bathroom right after she eats? Does she have bloodshot eyes, puffiness around her outer lips, or sunken cheeks? Does she brush her teeth a lot to get rid of bad breath? Your friend might be purging. Talk to her. Tell her you care and you are concerned about her well-being. And then talk to a trusted adult.

What type of research is being done to help people with ED?

A: Many different types of research are taking place—some of it with genetics, some with social issues, and others with psychological issues. ED is a complex web of different factors. There doesn't appear to be one simple answer that will solve the problem.

How do I find a good treatment program?

A: Your healthcare professional can recommend several places that can help with eating disorders. It's usually best to start with your family doctor.

Other Resources

There is a lot of information available for people suffering from eating disorders and their families and friends. However, you might find that a lot of the information repeats itself. You might also notice that some of it is not reliable. Here are some sources you should find helpful. The Web sites contain information that is useful in the United States and Canada. Telephone numbers and referral services are good in either the United States or Canada, but not both. If you do call a number outside of your area, the helpline will probably refer you to a number inside your region.

In Canada
Eating Disorders Coalition of Waterloo Region
www.edacwr.com/
Good information on eating disorders, body image, and dieting.

Canadian Mental Health Association: Facts About Eating Disorders
www.cmha.ca/mental_health/facts-about-eating-disorders/
Describes eating disorders and how they are associated with mental health.

Mind Your Mind

www.MindYourMind.ca

A site designed specifically for young people. It deals with many topics and gives you a place to talk with others about your situation and your feelings.

In the United States

Eating Disorders Online: Eating Disorders in Men

www.eatingdisordersonline.com/eating-disorders-in-men

This site provides concise, relevant information and a meeting place for those seeking a path to recovery.

KidsHealth.org

www.kidshealth.org/

KidsHealth.org provides information about various health-related topics that you can trust.

Hotlines in the United States

Anorexia and Associate Disorders
1-847-831-3438

National Mental Health Association
1-800-969-6642

Hotlines in Canada

Mental Health Helpline
1-866-531-2600

National Eating Disorder Information Help Centre
1-866-633-4220

KidsHelpPhone.ca
1-800-668-6868

Glossary

avoidant personality disorder a mental illness which prevents people from interacting socially

calories Units of energy

carbohydrates One of three elements of food that contain starch and sugar used by the body for energy

chromosome A thread of DNA that carries genes

chronic Something that lasts for a long time

circulatory system The part of the body made up of the heart and blood vessels

clavicle The slender bone that runs from your chest bone to your shoulder bone

constipation Unable to have a bowel movement

dehydration Loss of body fluid

diuretic Drug that increases the output of urine

enema A procedure in which a liquid is injected into the rectum to remove its contents

ephedrine Drug used in the treatment of asthma and allergies

esophagus The tube that connects the mouth to the stomach

ethnicity A group with common culture, nationality and background

flatulence Gas produced from digestion in the intestines and passed from the rectum

genes Units of inherited characteristics that determine the characteristics of an individual, such as eye and hair color

genetically predisposed Genetic influences

hydrochloric acid The type of acid in the stomach used to break down food

Ipecac Syrup that induces vomiting

laxatives Drugs or substances that promote bowel movements

menstrual Relating to the monthly discharge of blood and other matter from the womb

muscle dysmorphia A mental illness in which a person becomes preoccupied with not being muscular enough

obesity Increased body weight caused by excessive fat accumulation

obsessive-compulsive Behavior that is uncontrollable and repetitive

oppositional defiant disorder A pattern of aggressive behavior to those in authority.

purging To remove or cleanse

steroids Synthetic hormones that can boost the body's ability to produce muscle

undernourished Poor nutrition due to unbalanced eating

Index